ACADEMY AWARD® W
MOVIE POSTERS

volume three of
the illustrated history of movies through posters

Published by BRUCE HERSHENSON
P.O. Box 874, West Plains, MO 65775

Note: For the first six years, the Awards were given for a twelve month period that overlapped two calendar years. For the first year *only*, the Best Director Award was given in two categories, Drama and Comedy. Also, the Best Actor and Actress Awards were given for the performer's total output during the preceding twelve months. Thus Janet Gaynor won for the three films she had made, and Emil Jannings for the two he had made.

1, 2. WINGS, Best Picture, 1927/28, window card and set of eight lobby cards

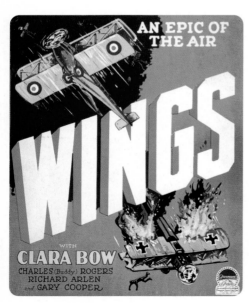

5. JANET GAYNOR, Best Actress, 7th Heaven, 1927/28, lobby card

3. WINGS, Best Picture, 1927/28, window card

4. FRANK BORZAGE, Best Director/ Drama, 7th Heaven, 1927/28, one-sheet

6. LEWIS MILESTONE, Best Director/ Comedy, Two Arabian Nights, 1927/28, lobby card

7. JANET GAYNOR, Best Actress,
Street Angel, 1927/28, one-sheet

8. EMIL JANNINGS, Best Actor, The Last
Command, 1927/28, window card

9. JANET GAYNOR, Best Actress, Sunrise,
1927/28, lobby card

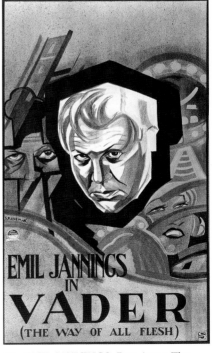

10. EMIL JANNINGS, Best Actor, The
Way of All Flesh, 1927/28, Dutch poster

11. THE BROADWAY MELODY, Best
Picture, 1928/29, special promotional poster

Note: It is easy to see the impact the
advent of sound had on movies by
looking at the posters of the winners
of the second Academy Awards.
Each makes absolutely sure the
audience knew they were about to
see a talking picture.

13. WARNER BAXTER, Best Actor, In Old
Arizona, 1928/29, one-sheet

14. MARY PICKFORD, Best Actress,
Coquette, 1928/29, window card

12. FRANK LLOYD, Best Director,
The Divine Lady, 1928/29, lobby card

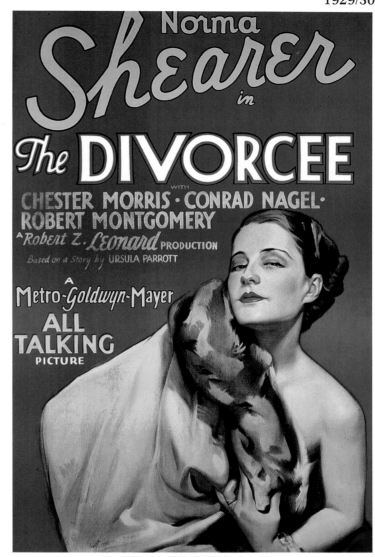

15. ALL QUIET ON THE WESTERN
FRONT, Best Picture, 1929/30, one-sheet

16. NORMA SHEARER, Best Actress,
The Divorcee, 1929/30, one-sheet

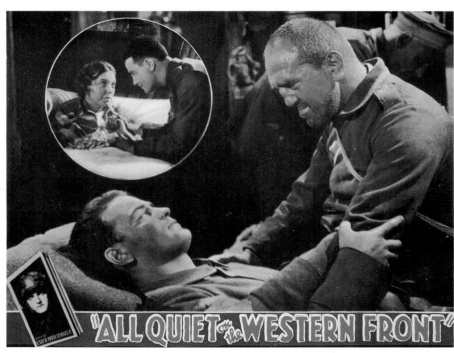

17. LEWIS MILESTONE, Best Director,
All Quiet on the Western Front, 1929/30,
lobby card

18. GEORGE ARLISS, Best Actor, Disraeli,
1929/30, one-sheet

19. CIMARRON, Best Picture, 1930/31,
Swedish poster

20. LIONEL BARRYMORE, Best Actor,
A Free Soul, 1930/31, still

Note: Lionel Barrymore was not the top-billed male performer in *A Free Soul,* and did not appear on the film's posters. Yet he was awarded the Best Actor Award. No doubt this helped lead the Academy to add Supporting Acting Awards (in 1936), so that superlative secondary performances would not have to compete against starring roles.

21. NORMAN TAUROG, Best Director,
Skippy, 1930/31, window card

22. MARIE DRESSLER, Best Actress,
Min and Bill, 1930/31, lobby card

23. GRAND HOTEL, Best Picture, 1931/32,
Belgian poster

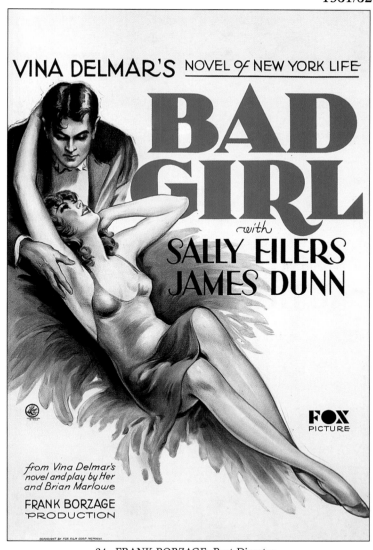

24. FRANK BORZAGE, Best Director,
Bad Girl, 1931/32, one-sheet

25. WALLACE BEERY, Best Actor (tie),
The Champ, 1931/32, one-sheet

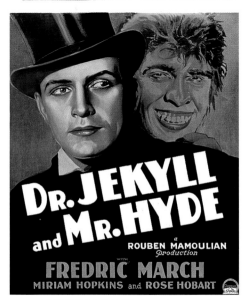

26. FREDRIC MARCH, Best Actor (tie),
Dr. Jekyll and Mr. Hyde, 1931/32, window
card

27. HELEN HAYES, Best Actress, The Sin of
Madelon Claudet, 1931/32, Swedish poster

28. CAVALCADE, Best Picture, 1932/33,
three-sheet

29. FRANK LLOYD, Best Director,
Cavalcade, 1932/33, lobby card

Note: *Cavalcade* was an English
film that was distributed in the
United States by Fox Film. It
would only be on very rare
occasions that the Academy
would give its highest award to
a foreign film.

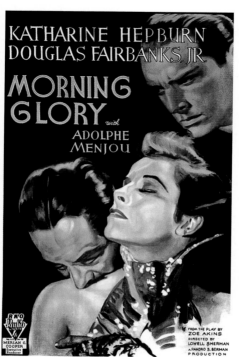

30. KATHARINE HEPBURN, Best Actress,
Morning Glory, 1932/33, one-sheet

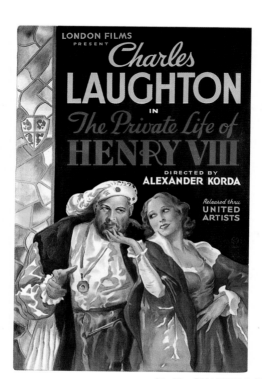

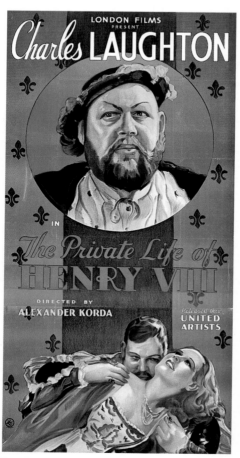

31, 32. CHARLES LAUGHTON, Best Actor,
The Private Life of Henry VIII, 1932/33,
one-sheet and three-sheet

Note: *It Happened One Night* was the first film to sweep the four major Awards (the Supporting Awards had not yet been added). This would not happen again for forty years.

33. IT HAPPENED ONE NIGHT,
Best Picture, 1934, one-sheet

34. FRANK CAPRA, Best Director, It
Happened One Night, 1934, window card

35. CLARK GABLE, Best Actor, It
Happened One Night, 1934, Belgian poster

36–39. CLAUDETTE COLBERT, Best
Actress, It Happened One Night, 1934,
four reissue lobby cards

40. MUTINY ON THE BOUNTY, Best
Picture, 1935, Danish poster

41. JOHN FORD, Best Director,
The Informer, 1935, three-sheet

42. MUTINY ON THE BOUNTY,
Best Picture, 1935, window card

43. BETTE DAVIS, Best Actress, Dangerous,
1935, one-sheet

44. VICTOR McLAGLEN, Best Actor,
The Informer, 1935, one-sheet

45. THE GREAT ZIEGFELD, Best Picture,
1936, one-sheet

46. FRANK CAPRA, Best Director,
Mr. Deeds Goes to Town, 1936, one-sheet

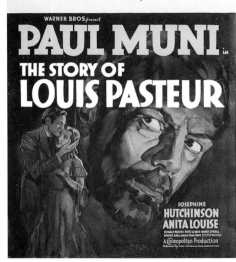

Note: The Academy added Best Supporting
Actor and Actress Awards in 1936. This
would be the last substantial change in the
Awards system. Strangely, Luise Rainer won
the Best Actress Award for what was
essentially a supporting role.

49. WALTER BRENNAN, Best Supporting
Actor, Come and Get It, 1936, still

47. PAUL MUNI, Best Actor, The Story of
Louis Pasteur, 1936, window card

48. LUISE RAINER, Best Actress,
The Great Ziegfeld, 1936, still

50. GALE SONDERGAARD, Best Supporting
Actress, Anthony Adverse, 1936, lobby card

51. THE LIFE OF EMILE ZOLA,
Best Picture, 1937, one-sheet

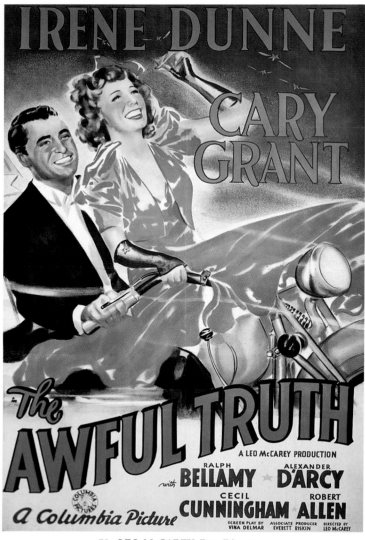

52. LEO McCAREY, Best Director,
The Awful Truth, 1937, one-sheet

53. SPENCER TRACY, Best Actor,
Captains Courageous, 1937, one-sheet

54. LUISE RAINER, Best Actress,
The Good Earth, 1937, one-sheet

55. JOSEPH SCHILDKRAUT, Best Supporting
Actor, The Life of Emile Zola, 1937, still

56. ALICE BRADY, Best Supporting
Actress, In Old Chicago, 1937, lobby card

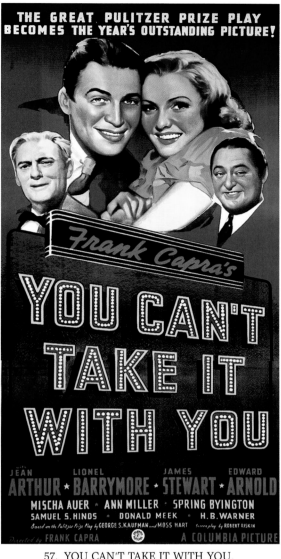

57. YOU CAN'T TAKE IT WITH YOU, Best Picture, 1938, three-sheet

58. BETTE DAVIS, Best Actress, Jezebel, 1938, one-sheet

61. FAY BAINTER, Best Supporting Actress, Jezebel, 1938, lobby card

59. FRANK CAPRA, Best Director, You Can't Take It With You, 1938, one-sheet

60. SPENCER TRACY, Best Actor, Boys Town, 1938, one-sheet

62. WALTER BRENNAN, Best Supporting Actor, Kentucky, 1938, lobby card

63. GONE WITH THE WIND,
Best Picture, 1939, six-sheet

Note: Many, many people feel that *Gone With the Wind* should have swept the Oscars (including the Supporting Awards). But Clark Gable had already won the Best Actor Award and it seems that a general feeling had developed within the Academy that the Awards should be spread around (especially after the back-to-back wins of Luise Rainer and Spencer Tracy). This attitude seemed to prevail (with a few exceptions) until the demise of the studio system in the 1970s.

64. VICTOR FLEMING, Best Director,
Gone with the Wind, 1939, half-sheet

65. ROBERT DONAT, Best Actor, Goodbye
Mr. Chips, 1939, one-sheet

66. VIVIEN LEIGH, Best Actress,
Gone with the Wind, 1939, insert

67. HATTIE McDANIEL, Best Supporting
Actress, Gone with the Wind, 1939, lobby
card

68. THOMAS MITCHELL, Best Supporting
Actor, Stagecoach, 1939, lobby card

69. JOHN FORD, Best Director, The
Grapes of Wrath, 1940, Forty By Sixty

70. REBECCA, Best Picture, 1940,
half-sheet

71. WALTER BRENNAN, Best Supporting
Actor, The Westerner, 1940, lobby card

72. JANE DARWELL, Best Supporting Actress,
The Grapes of Wrath, 1940, lobby card

73. GINGER ROGERS, Best Actress,
Kitty Foyle, 1940, one-sheet

74. JOHN FORD, Best Director, The
Grapes of Wrath, 1940, Title lobby card

75. JAMES STEWART, Best Actor, The
Philadelphia Story, 1940, lobby card

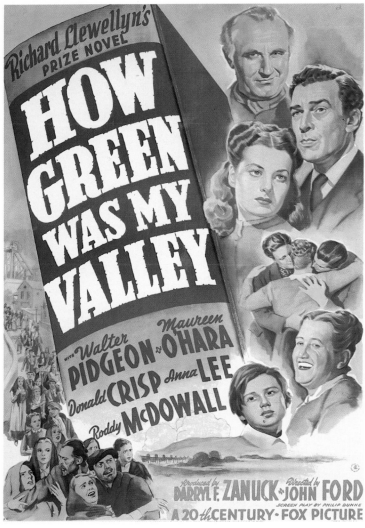

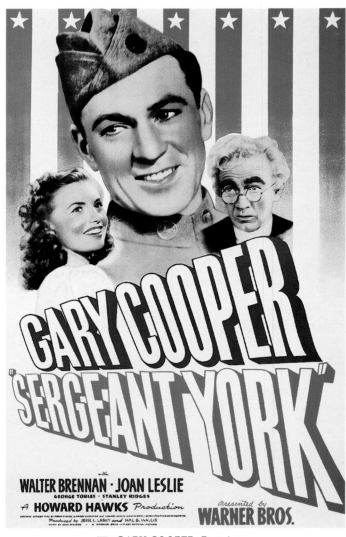

76. HOW GREEN WAS MY VALLEY,
Best Picture, 1941, one-sheet

77. GARY COOPER, Best Actor,
Sergeant York, 1941, one-sheet

80. DONALD CRISP, Best Supporting
Actor, How Green Was My Valley, 1941,
lobby card

78. JOAN FONTAINE, Best Actress,
Suspicion, 1941, three-sheet

79. JOHN FORD, Best Director, How
Green Was My Valley, 1941, French poster

81. MARY ASTOR, Best Supporting
Actress, The Great Lie, 1941, lobby card

82. MRS. MINIVER, Best Picture,
also WILLIAM WYLER, Best Director,
1942, one-sheet

83. GREER GARSON, Best Actress,
Mrs. Miniver, 1942, French poster

Note: Van Heflin was sixth-billed and not
pictured on the posters originally issued for
Johnny Eager in 1942. However, after he won
the Best Supporting Actor Award, the film
was reissued several years later with Heflin
receiving equal billing to Taylor and Turner.

84. JAMES CAGNEY, Best Actor, Yankee
Doodle Dandy, 1942, six-sheet

85. VAN HEFLIN, Best Supporting
Actor, Johnny Eager, 1942, reissue
insert

86. TERESA WRIGHT, Best Supporting
Actress, Mrs. Miniver, 1942, lobby card

87. CASABLANCA, Best Picture, 1943,
Title lobby card

Note: *Casablanca* could certainly have swept the top four Awards. In what was to become a common Oscar event, Ingrid Bergman received the Best Actress Award the following year, perhaps in part to make up for her not having won for *Casablanca*. It wasn't until eight more years had passed that Humphrey Bogart finally received his long overdue Best Actor Award.

88. MICHAEL CURTIZ, Best Director, Casablanca, 1943, insert

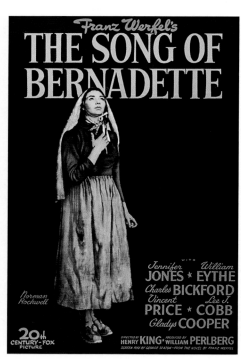

89. JENNIFER JONES, Best Actress, The Song of Bernadette, 1943, one-sheet

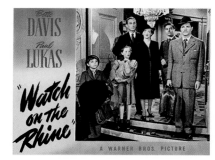

90. PAUL LUKAS, Best Actor, Watch on the Rhine, 1943, lobby card

91. CHARLES COBURN, Best Supporting Actor, The More the Merrier, 1943, lobby card

92. KATINA PAXINOU, Best Supporting Actress, For Whom the Bell Tolls, 1943, one-sheet

93. GOING MY WAY, Best Picture, 1944,
lobby card

94. LEO McCAREY, Best Director,
Going My Way, 1944, lobby card

95. BING CROSBY, Best Actor, Going My
Way, 1944, one-sheet

96. INGRID BERGMAN, Best Actress,
Gaslight, 1944, one-sheet

Note: It seems that Paramount
Pictures was reluctant to pro-
mote *Going My Way* as a film
about the relationship between
a gruff older priest and a brash
younger one. The poster for the
film shows Bing Crosby in
ambiguous clothing, apparently
out on a date! Fortunately, the
film was a huge critical and
commercial success in spite of
the misleading ad campaign.

97. BARRY FITZGERALD, Best Supporting
Actor, Going My Way, 1944, lobby card

98. ETHEL BARRYMORE, Best Supporting
Actress, None But the Lonely Heart, 1944,
lobby card

99. THE LOST WEEKEND, Best Picture,
also BILLY WILDER, Best Director, 1945,
lobby card

100. RAY MILLAND, Best Actor, The Lost
Weekend, 1945, French poster

101. JOAN CRAWFORD, Best Actress,
Mildred Pierce, 1945, Italian poster

102. JAMES DUNN, Best Supporting Actor,
A Tree Grows in Brooklyn, 1945, lobby card

103. ANN REVERE, Best Supporting
Actress, National Velvet, 1945, lobby card

104. THE BEST YEARS OF OUR LIVES,
Best Picture,
also WILLIAM WYLER, Best Director,
1946, Title lobby card

Note: *The Best Years of Our Lives* had a major subplot that centered
around a veteran who had lost his hands in World War II (played by
real-life veteran Harold Russell, who deservedly won the Best Supporting
Actor Award). Yet the producers of the film virtually shut Russell out of
the film's advertising, perhaps worried about "shocking" the public.

106. OLIVIA de HAVILLAND, Best Actress,
To Each His Own, 1946, Spanish poster

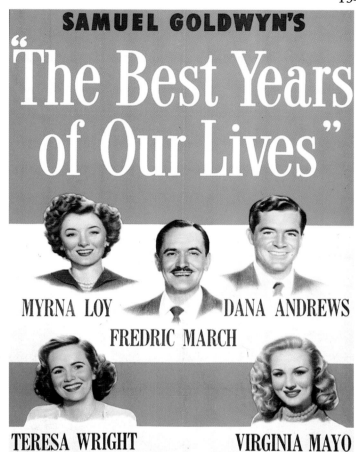

105. FREDRIC MARCH, Best Actor, The
Best Years of Our Lives, 1946, one-sheet

107. HAROLD RUSSELL, Best Supporting
Actor, The Best Years of Our Lives, 1946, still

108. ANNE BAXTER, Best Supporting
Actress, The Razor's Edge, 1946, lobby card

109. GENTLEMAN'S AGREEMENT,
Best Picture, 1947, three-sheet

110. ELIA KAZAN, Best Director,
Gentleman's Agreement, 1947, one-sheet

111. RONALD COLMAN, Best Actor,
A Double Life, 1947, three-sheet

112. LORETTA YOUNG, Best Actress,
The Farmer's Daughter, 1947, one-sheet

113. CELESTE HOLM, Best Supporting Actress,
Gentleman's Agreement, 1947, lobby card

114. EDMUND GWENN, Best Supporting
Actor, Miracle on 34th Street, 1947, lobby card

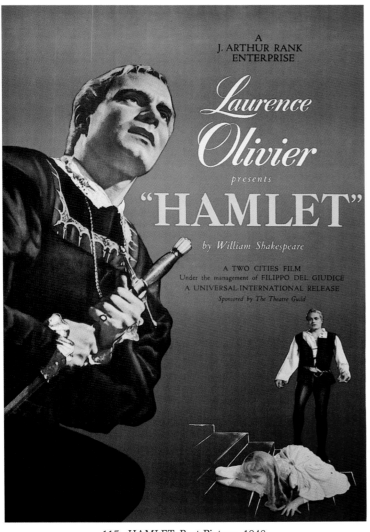

115. HAMLET, Best Picture, 1948, one-sheet

116. JOHN HUSTON, Best Director, The Treasure of the Sierra Madre, 1948, French poster

117. LAURENCE OLIVIER, Best Actor, Hamlet, 1948, lobby card

118. CLAIRE TREVOR, Best Supporting Actress, Key Largo, 1948, British quad poster

119. JANE WYMAN, Best Actress, Johnny Belinda, 1948, one-sheet

120. WALTER HUSTON, Best Supporting Actor, The Treasure of the Sierra Madre, 1948, one-sheet

121. ALL THE KING'S MEN, Best Picture, *also* BRODERICK CRAWFORD, Best Actor, 1949, Title lobby card

Note: *All the King's Men* won three of the top six Oscars, including Best Picture, yet the film was given the most uninspired advertising campaign of any Best Picture winner. As a result, the posters on this film are extremely difficult to find, as few collectors ever bothered to save them.

122. JOSEPH L. MANKIEWICZ, Best Director, A Letter to Three Wives, 1949, one-sheet

123. OLIVIA de HAVILLAND, Best Actress, The Heiress, 1949, lobby card

124. DEAN JAGGER, Best Supporting Actor, Twelve O'Clock High, 1949, lobby card

125. MERCEDES McCAMBRIDGE, Best Supporting Actress, All the King's Men, 1949, lobby card

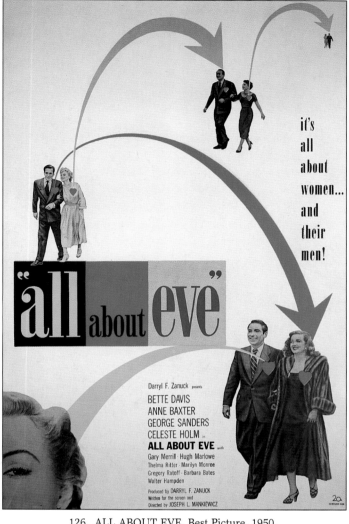

126. ALL ABOUT EVE, Best Picture, 1950,
one-sheet

127, 128. JOSEPH MANKIEWICZ, Best
Director, All About Eve, 1950, two lobby
cards

132. GEORGE SANDERS, Best Supporting
Actor, All About Eve, 1950, lobby card

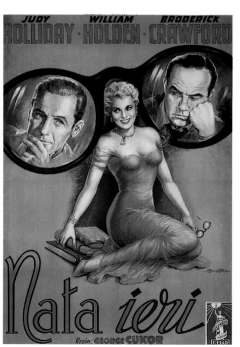

129, 130. JOSE FERRER, Best Actor,
Cyrano de Bergerac, 1950, two lobby cards

131. JUDY HOLLIDAY, Best Actress,
Born Yesterday, 1950, Italian poster

133. JOSEPHINE HILL, Best Supporting
Actress, Harvey, 1950, lobby card

134. AN AMERICAN IN PARIS, Best Picture, 1951, three-sheet

135, 136. GEORGE STEVENS, Best Director, A Place in the Sun, 1951, two lobby cards

137. HUMPHREY BOGART, Best Actor, The African Queen, 1951, British poster

Note: Few actors have ever had as strong an impact on both the critics and the public as Marlon Brando in *A Streetcar Named Desire*. Yet he was denied the Best Actor Award, probably because the person who did win, Humphrey Bogart, had been unfairly passed over many times. While Bogart gave a marvelous performance in *The African Queen*, Brando was probably more deserving. The Academy probably reasoned that Bogart was nearing the end of his career while Brando was only beginning his and that gave the edge to Bogart.

139. KARL MALDEN, Best Supporting Actor, A Streetcar Named Desire, 1951, still

138. VIVIEN LEIGH, Best Actress, A Streetcar Named Desire, 1951, lobby card

140. KIM HUNTER, Best Supporting Actress, A Streetcar Named Desire, 1951, lobby reissue card

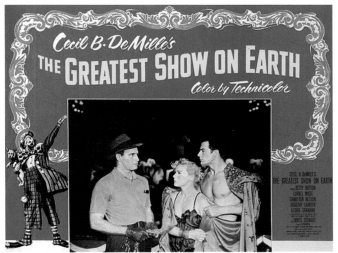

143. JOHN FORD, Best Director, The Quiet Man, 1952, six-sheet

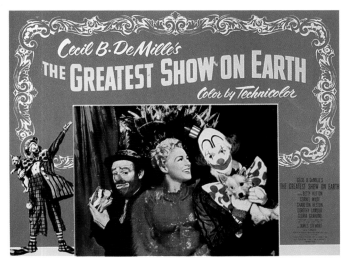

141, 142. THE GREATEST SHOW ON EARTH, Best Picture, 1952, two lobby cards

Note: 1952 illustrates another basic trend in the awarding of Academy Awards. When deciding on the recipient of the Best Picture Award, the Academy almost always chooses a big budget, non-controversial film such as *The Greatest Show on Earth* over smaller, highly personal movies such as *The Quiet Man* or *High Noon,* even though many people feel the smaller films are often far more deserving.

144. GARY COOPER, Best Actor, High Noon, 1952, Italian poster

145. SHIRLEY BOOTH, Best Actress, Come Back, Little Sheba, 1952, one-sheet

146. ANTHONY QUINN, Best Supporting Actor, Viva Zapata, 1952, lobby card

147. GLORIA GRAHAME, Best Supporting Actress, The Bad and the Beautiful, 1952, lobby card

148. FROM HERE TO ETERNITY, Best
Picture, 1953, Italian poster

149. FRED ZINNEMANN, Best Director,
From Here to Eternity, 1953, Danish poster

150, 151. WILLIAM HOLDEN, Best Actor,
Stalag 17, 1953, two lobby cards

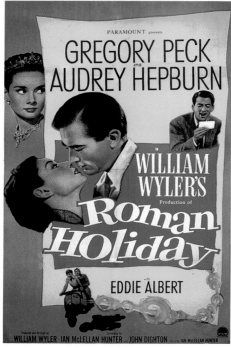

152. AUDREY HEPBURN, Best Actress,
Roman Holiday, 1953, one-sheet

Note: By the 1950s, the general
artistic quality of American posters
had declined drastically. Quite often,
the posters were simply photo
montages. Many collectors feel that
posters for the foreign release of
films of this period frequently out-
shine their American counterparts.

153. FRANK SINATRA, Best Supporting
Actor, From Here to Eternity, 1953,
also DONNA REED, Best Supporting
Actress, lobby card

154. ON THE WATERFRONT, Best Picture, 1954, Italian poster

155. ELIA KAZAN, Best Director, On the Waterfront, 1954, lobby card

Note: In 1954, *On the Waterfront* won all but one of the top Academy Awards it was eligible for (it had no performance by a female in a leading role). The Academy gave the Best Supporting Actor Award to Edmond O'Brien over Rod Steiger, who gave one of the cinema's most memorable performances. One hopes that the Academy recognized that a star of Steiger's magnitude and range would almost certainly receive an Award in the future.

156. MARLON BRANDO, Best Actor, On the Waterfront, 1954, Italian poster

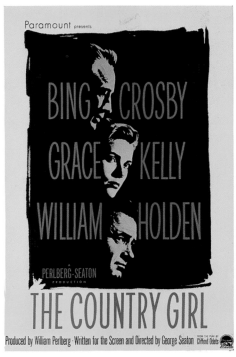

157. GRACE KELLY, Best Actress, The Country Girl, 1954, one-sheet

158. EDMUND O'BRIEN, Best Supporting Actor, The Barefoot Contessa, 1954, still

159. EVA MARIE SAINT, Best Supporting Actress, On the Waterfront, 1954, lobby card

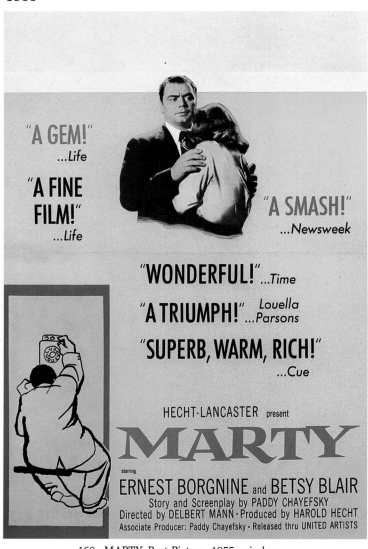

161. DELBERT MANN, Best Director,
Marty, 1955, lobby card

162. ERNEST BORGNINE, Best Actor,
Marty, 1955, lobby card

160. MARTY, Best Picture, 1955, window
card

163, 164. ANNA MAGNANI, Best Actress,
The Rose Tattoo, 1955, two lobby cards

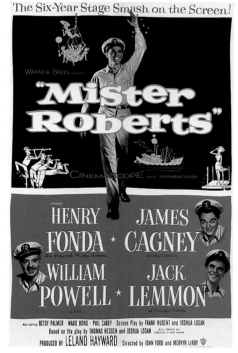

165. JACK LEMMON, Best Supporting
Actor, Mister Roberts, 1955, one-sheet

166. JO VAN FLEET, Best Supporting Actress,
East of Eden, 1955, Italian photobusta

167, 168. AROUND THE WORLD IN 80 DAYS, Best Picture, 1956, two lobby cards

169. GEORGE STEVENS, Best Director, Giant, 1956, Forty By Sixty

170. YUL BRYNNER, Best Actor, The King and I, 1956, still

171. INGRID BERGMAN, Best Actress, Anastasia, 1956, one-sheet

172. ANTHONY QUINN, Best Supporting Actor, Lust for Life, 1956, lobby card

173. DOROTHY MALONE, Best Supporting Actress, Written on the Wind, 1956, lobby card

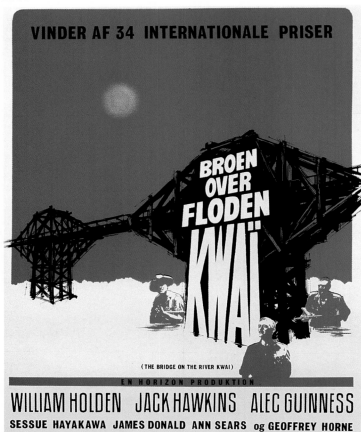

VINDER AF 34 INTERNATIONALE PRISER

BROEN OVER FLODEN KWAÏ

(THE BRIDGE ON THE RIVER KWAI)

EN HORIZON PRODUKTION

WILLIAM HOLDEN   JACK HAWKINS   ALEC GUINNESS

SESSUE HAYAKAWA   JAMES DONALD   ANN SEARS   og GEOFFREY HORNE

PRODUCERET AF SAM SPIEGEL   Manuskript af PIERRE BOULLE
Iscenesat af DAVID LEAN   TECHNICOLOR   CINEMASCOPE   efter hans egen roman

174. THE BRIDGE ON THE RIVER KWAI,
Best Picture, 1957, Danish poster

175. ALEC GUINNESS, Best Actor, The
Bridge on the River Kwai, 1957, lobby card

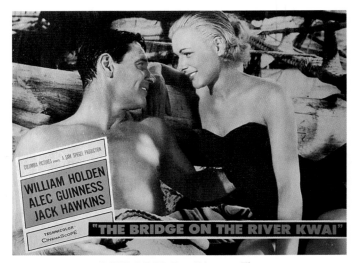

176. DAVID LEAN, Best Director, The
Bridge on the River Kwai, 1957, lobby card

THE STRANGEST TRUE EXPERIENCE A YOUNG GIRL IN LOVE EVER LIVED!

20. Century-Fox presents

The Three Faces Of Eve

JOANNE WOODWARD · DAVID WAYNE · LEE J. COBB

CINEMASCOPE   NUNNALLY JOHNSON

177. JOANNE WOODWARD, Best Actress,
The Three Faces of Eve, 1957, one-sheet

MARLON BRANDO IN SAYONARA TECHNIRAMA and TECHNICOLOR presented by WARNER BROS.

178. RED BUTTONS, Best Supporting
Actor, Sayonara, 1957,
also MIYOSHI UMEKI, Best Supporting
Actress, lobby card

179. GIGI, Best Picture, 1958, one-sheet

180, 181. VINCENTE MINNELLI, Best
Director, Gigi, 1958, two lobby cards

Note: In 1958 the Best Actor Oscar
was strangely given to David Niven,
a well-liked and distinguished actor.
While he gave his usual strong performance in *Separate Tables,* he
clearly played a supporting role.
Perhaps his award was more of a
lifetime achievement award.

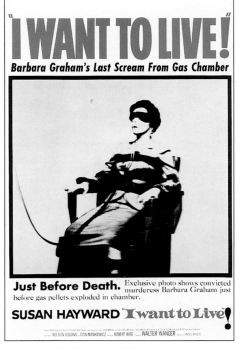

184. BURL IVES, Best Supporting Actor,
The Big Country, 1958, lobby card

182. DAVID NIVEN, Best Actor,
Separate Tables, 1958, lobby card

183. SUSAN HAYWARD, Best Actress,
I Want to Live, 1958, one-sheet

185. WENDY HILLER, Best Supporting
Actress, Separate Tables, 1958, lobby card

186. BEN-HUR, Best Picture, 1959, one-sheet

187, 188. WILLIAM WYLER, Best Director, Ben-Hur, 1959, two lobby cards

189, 190. CHARLTON HESTON, Best Actor, Ben-Hur, 1959, two lobby cards

191. SIMONE SIGNORET, Best Actress, Room at the Top, 1959, one-sheet

192. HUGH GRIFFITH, Best Supporting Actor, Ben-Hur, 1959, lobby card

193. SHELLEY WINTERS, Best Supporting Actor, The Diary of Anne Frank, 1959, lobby card

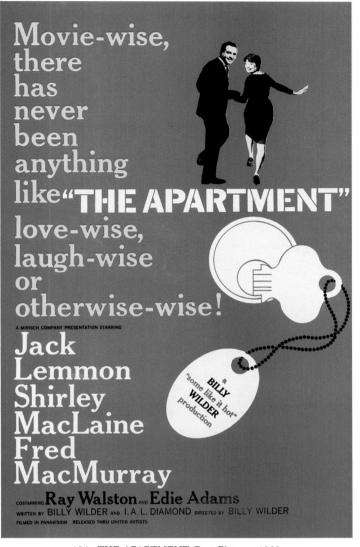

194. THE APARTMENT, Best Picture, 1960,
one-sheet

195. ELIZABETH TAYLOR, Best Actress,
Butterfield 8, 1960, British quad poster

Note: 1960 marked a turning point in the motion picture industry's willingness to confront adult situations. All of the movies that won the top Awards dealt frankly and candidly with subjects that would have been avoided by mainstream film makers only a few years prior.

199. PETER USTINOV, Best Supporting
Actor, Spartacus, 1960, lobby card

196, 197. BILLY WILDER, Best Director,
The Apartment, 1960, two lobby cards

198. BURT LANCASTER, Best Actor, Elmer
Gantry, 1960, one-sheet

200. SHIRLEY JONES, Best Supporting
Actress, Elmer Gantry, 1960, lobby card

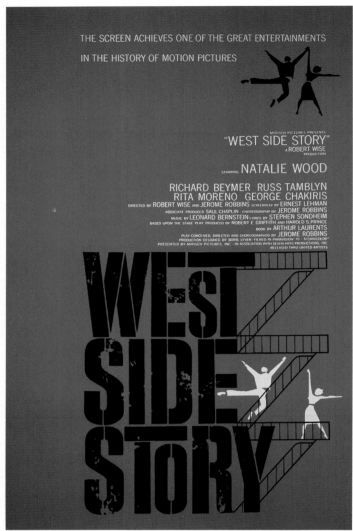

201. WEST SIDE STORY, Best Picture,
1961, one-sheet

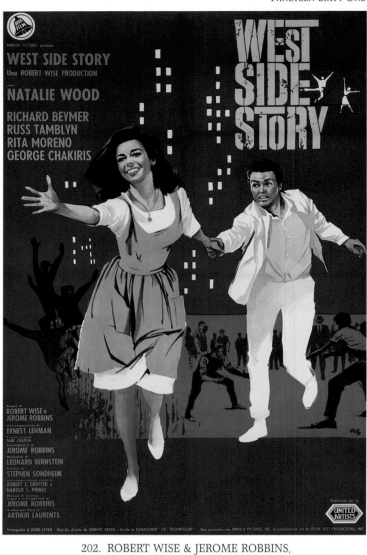

202. ROBERT WISE & JEROME ROBBINS,
Best Directors, West Side Story, 1961,
reissue Italian poster

203. MAXIMILLIAN SCHELL, Best Actor,
Judgement at Nurenberg, 1961, one-sheet

204. SOPHIA LOREN, Best Actress,
Two Women, 1961, one-sheet

205. GEORGE CHAKIRIS, Best Supporting
Actor, West Side Story, 1961, lobby card

206. RITA MORENO, Best Supporting
Actress, West Side Story, 1961, lobby card

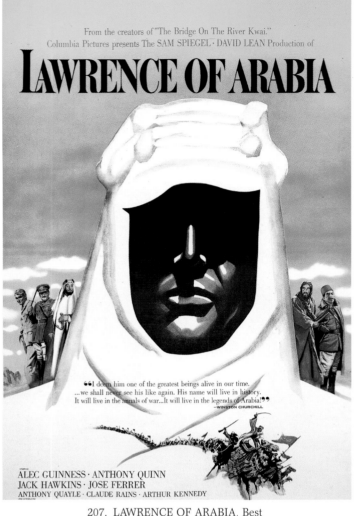

207. LAWRENCE OF ARABIA, Best Picture, 1962, one-sheet

208. DAVID LEAN, Best Director, Lawrence of Arabia, 1962, pressbook cover

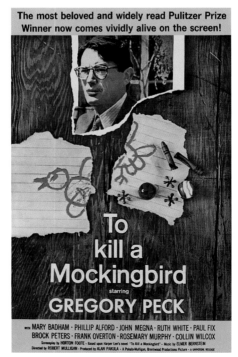

209. GREGORY PECK, Best Actor, To Kill a Mockingbird, 1962, one-sheet

210. ANNE BANCROFT, Best Actress, The Miracle Worker, 1962, one-sheet

211. ED BEGLEY, Best Supporting Actor, Sweet Bird of Youth, 1962, lobby card

212. PATTY DUKE, Best Supporting Actress, The Miracle Worker, 1962, lobby card

213. TOM JONES, Best Picture, 1963, one-sheet

214. TONY RICHARDSON, Best Director, Tom Jones, 1963, lobby card

215. PATRICIA NEAL, Best Actress, Hud, 1963, lobby card

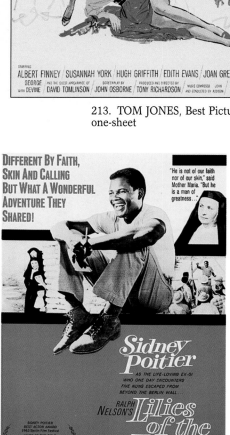

216. SIDNEY POITIER, Best Actor, Lilies of the Field, 1963, one-sheet

217. MELVYN DOUGLAS, Best Supporting Actor, Hud, 1963, lobby card

218. MARGARET RUTHERFORD, Best Supporting Actress, The V.I.P.s, 1963, lobby card

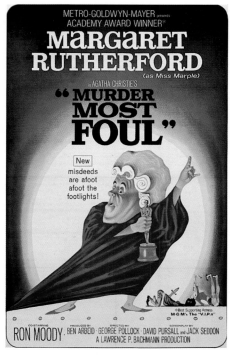

219. MARGARET RUTHERFORD, Murder Most Foul, one-sheet, showing her holding her Oscar from The V.I.P.s!

220. MY FAIR LADY, Best Picture, 1964, one-sheet

221, 222. GEORGE CUKOR, Best Director, My Fair Lady, 1964, lobby card and Italian photobusta

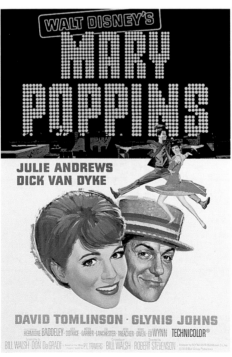

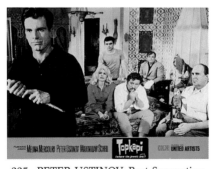

225. PETER USTINOV, Best Supporting Actor, Topkapi, 1964, lobby card

223. REX HARRISON, Best Actor, My Fair Lady, 1964, Italian poster

224. JULIE ANDREWS, Best Actress, Mary Poppins, 1964, one-sheet

226. LILA KEDROVA, Best Supporting Actress, Zorba the Greek, 1964, lobby card

227. THE SOUND OF MUSIC, Best Picture, 1965, still

228, 229. ROBERT WISE, Best Director, The Sound of Music, 1965, lobby card and still

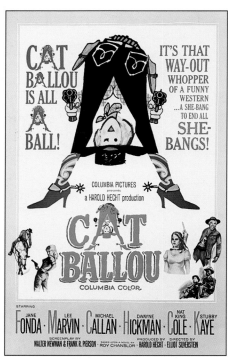

230. LEE MARVIN, Best Actor, Cat Ballou, 1965, one-sheet

231. JULIE CHRISTIE, Best Actress, Darling, 1965, one-sheet

232. MARTIN BALSAM, Best Supporting Actor, A Thousand Clowns, 1965, still

233. SHELLEY WINTERS, Best Supporting Actress, A Patch of Blue, 1965, lobby card

234. A MAN FOR ALL SEASONS, Best Picture,
also FRED ZINNEMANN, Best Director, 1966,
one-sheet

235. PAUL SCOFIELD, Best Actor, A Man
for All Seasons, 1966, "awards" one-sheet

236. ELIZABETH TAYLOR, Best Actress,
Who's Afraid of Virginia Woolf?, 1966,
also SANDY DENNIS, Best Supporting
Actress, lobby card

237. WALTER MATTHAU, Best Supporting
Actor, The Fortune Cookie, 1966, one-sheet

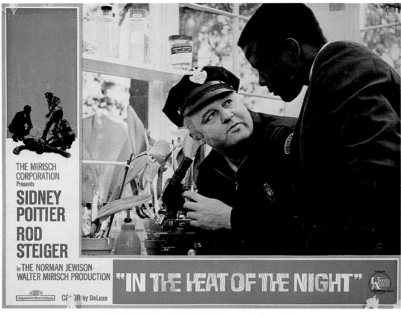

238. IN THE HEAT OF THE NIGHT,
Best Picture, 1967, lobby card

Note: The 1967 Best Actor Award posed a dilemma for Academy voters.
Spencer Tracy died after filming *Guess Who's Coming To Dinner*, which
might have guaranteed an Oscar for this distinguished actor. However,
Rod Steiger had never been chosen, despite superlative performances in
such films as *On the Waterfront* and *The Pawnbroker*. Since Tracy had
received two Best Actor Awards early in his career, Steiger won the Oscar.

239, 240. MIKE NICHOLS, Best Director,
The Graduate, 1967, two lobby cards

244. GEORGE KENNEDY, Best Supporting
Actor, Cool Hand Luke, 1967, lobby card

241. ROD STEIGER, Best Actor, In the
Heat of the Night, 1967, one-sheet

242, 243. KATHARINE HEPBURN, Best
Actress, Guess Who's Coming to Dinner,
1967, two lobby cards

245. ESTELLE PARSONS, Best Supporting
Actress, Bonnie & Clyde, 1967, still

246. OLIVER!, Best Picture,
also CAROL REED, Best Director, 1968,
"awards" one-sheet

247. CLIFF ROBERTSON, Best Actor,
Charly, 1968, one-sheet

250. JACK ALBERTSON, Best Supporting
Actor, The Subject Was Roses, 1968,
lobby card

248. KATHARINE HEPBURN, Best Actress
(tie), The Lion in Winter, 1968, one-sheet

249. BARBRA STREISAND, Best Actress (tie),
Funny Girl, 1968, Spanish poster

251. RUTH GORDON, Best Supporting
Actress, Rosemary's Baby, 1968, still

252. MIDNIGHT COWBOY, Best Picture,
1969, one-sheet

253. JOHN WAYNE, Best Actor, True Grit,
1969, lobby card

Note: Perhaps the finest performance ever by a male actor in a leading role was given by Dustin Hoffman in *Midnight Cowboy*. Unfortunately, several factors combined to deny him the Best Actor Award. First, John Wayne, one of the cinema's greatest legends had never won an Oscar and had starred in *True Grit*. Second, Jon Voight, Hoffman's co-star, gave a performance that nearly equalled Hoffman's and Voight surely took some votes that would have gone to Hoffman. Third, *Midnight Cowboy*, with its X-rated homosexual theme was surely distasteful to many Academy voters. It is an Award such as this that points up the inherent weaknesses in the entire method of choosing Oscars.

256. GIG YOUNG, Best Supporting Actor,
They Shoot Horses, Don't They?, 1969,
lobby card

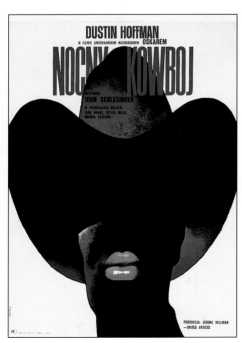

254. JOHN SCHLESINGER, Best Director,
Midnight Cowboy, 1969, Polish poster

255. MAGGIE SMITH, Best Actress, The
Prime of Miss Jean Brodie, 1969, one-sheet

257. GOLDIE HAWN, Best Supporting
Actress, Cactus Flower, 1969, lobby card

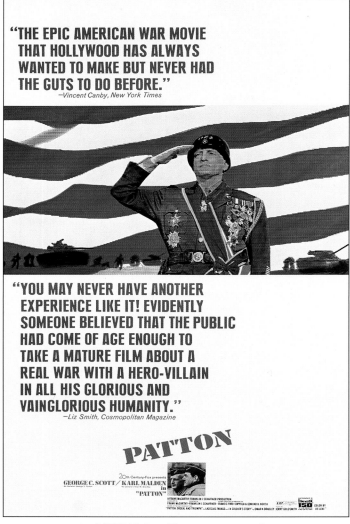

"THE EPIC AMERICAN WAR MOVIE
THAT HOLLYWOOD HAS ALWAYS
WANTED TO MAKE BUT NEVER HAD
THE GUTS TO DO BEFORE."
—Vincent Canby, New York Times

"YOU MAY NEVER HAVE ANOTHER
EXPERIENCE LIKE IT! EVIDENTLY
SOMEONE BELIEVED THAT THE PUBLIC
HAD COME OF AGE ENOUGH TO
TAKE A MATURE FILM ABOUT A
REAL WAR WITH A HERO-VILLAIN
IN ALL HIS GLORIOUS AND
VAINGLORIOUS HUMANITY."
—Liz Smith, Cosmopolitan Magazine

PATTON

258. PATTON, Best Picture, 1970, one-sheet

259. FRANKLIN J. SCHAFFNER,
Best Director, Patton, 1970, still

260. GEORGE C. SCOTT, Best Actor,
Patton, 1970, still

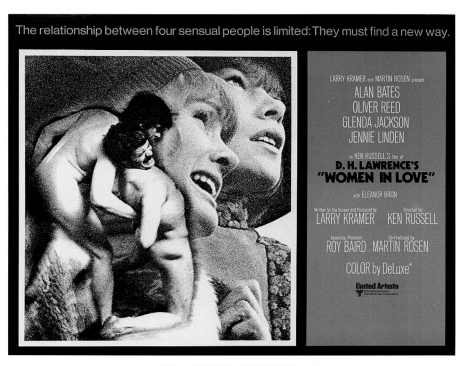

The relationship between four sensual people is limited: They must find a new way.

LARRY KRAMER and MARTIN ROSEN present

ALAN BATES
OLIVER REED
GLENDA JACKSON
JENNIE LINDEN

in KEN RUSSELL'S film of
D. H. LAWRENCE'S
"WOMEN IN LOVE"

with ELEANOR BRON

Written for the Screen and Produced by   Directed by
LARRY KRAMER   KEN RUSSELL

Associate Producer   Co-Produced by
ROY BAIRD   MARTIN ROSEN

COLOR by DeLuxe®

United Artists

261. GLENDA JACKSON, Best Actress,
Women in Love, 1970, half-sheet

"RYAN'S DAUGHTER"

262. JOHN MILLS, Best Supporting Actor,
Ryan's Daughter, 1970, lobby card

AIRPORT

263. HELEN HAYES, Best Supporting
Actress, Airport, 1970, lobby card

Doyle is
bad news—
but a
good
cop.

The time is just right for an out and out thriller like this.

THE FRENCH CONNECTION

20TH CENTURY-FOX PRESENTS "THE FRENCH CONNECTION" A PHILIP D'ANTONI PRODUCTION
STARRING GENE HACKMAN FERNANDO REY ROY SCHEIDER TONY LO BIANCO MARCEL BOZZUFFI
DIRECTED BY WILLIAM FRIEDKIN PRODUCED BY PHILIP D'ANTONI ASSOCIATE PRODUCER KENNETH UTT
EXECUTIVE PRODUCER G.DAVID SCHINE SCREENPLAY BY ERNEST TIDYMAN MUSIC COMPOSED AND CONDUCTED BY DON ELLIS
COLOR BY DE LUXE®

Note: *The French Connection* was a chase-filled crime thriller, a type of film the Academy hardly ever rewards with even a single Oscar. Yet it won Best Picture, Director, and Actor. No doubt this was due to the stylish direction of William Friedkin and the marvelous performance (as usual) by Gene Hackman, which resulted in a film that many consider the finest of its genre. In a surprising move, the posters for the film reveal the climax of the film's most exciting chase sequence.

THE FRENCH CONNECTION   Color by DE LUXE®   71/316

264. THE FRENCH CONNECTION,
Best Picture,
also WILLIAM FRIEDKIN, Best Director,
1971, one-sheet

265. GENE HACKMAN, Best Actor, The
French Connection, 1971, lobby card

jane fonda · donald sutherland

Lots
of guys
swing with
a call girl
like Bree.

One guy just
wants to
kill her.

an alan j. pakula production
'klute'

an alan j. pakula production starring jane fonda · donald sutherland in "klute" co-starring charles cioffi
nathan george · dorothy tristan · roy r. scheider · rita gam · music by michael small · written by andy
and dave lewis · co-produced by david lange · produced and directed by alan j. pakula · panavision ®
technicolor ® from warner bros...a kinney leisure service

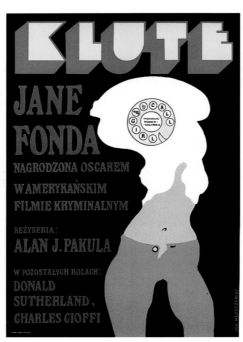

KLUTE

JANE
FONDA

NAGRODZONA OSCAREM

W AMERYKAŃSKIM
FILMIE KRYMINALNYM

REŻYSERIA:
ALAN J. PAKULA

W POZOSTAŁYCH ROLACH:
DONALD
SUTHERLAND,
CHARLES CIOFFI

THE PICTURE SHOW THAT
INTRODUCED AMERICA TO
THE FORGOTTEN 50'S.

It launched
the meteoric career
of its brilliant new
director and its
talented cast.

It won 2
Academy Awards,
and nominations for 8.

If you missed it
the first time, you owe
it to yourself now.

If you saw it once,
remember again.

COLUMBIA PICTURES
Presents
A BBS PRODUCTION

THE
LAST
PICTURE
SHOW

A film by
PETER BOGDANOVICH

STARRING TIMOTHY BOTTOMS·JEFF BRIDGES·ELLEN BURSTYN·BEN JOHNSON·CLORIS LEACHMAN·CYBILL SHEPHERD
DIRECTED BY PETER BOGDANOVICH·LARRY McMURTRY AND PETER BOGDANOVICH·PRODUCED BY BERT SCHNEIDER·STEPHEN J. FRIEDMAN

266, 267. JANE FONDA, Best Actress,
Klute, 1971, one-sheet and Polish poster

268. BEN JOHNSON, Best Supporting
Actor, The Last Picture Show, 1971,
also CLORIS LEACHMAN, Best Supporting
Actress, reissue one-sheet

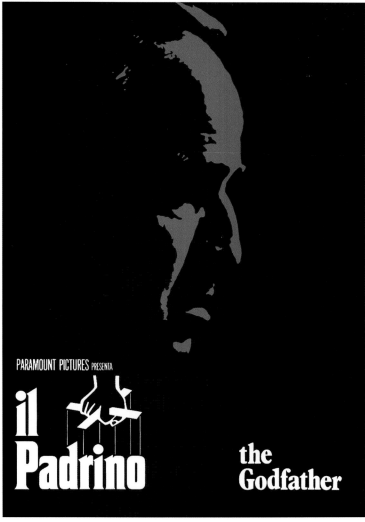

269. THE GODFATHER, Best Picture,
1972, Italian poster

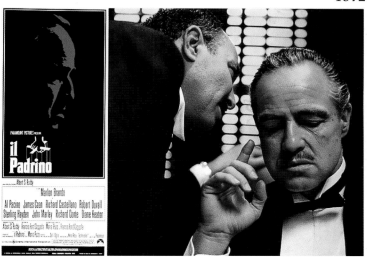

270. MARLON BRANDO, Best Actor,
The Godfather, 1972, Italian photobusta

271. EILEEN HECKART, Best Supporting
Actress, Butterflies Are Free, 1972, lobby
card

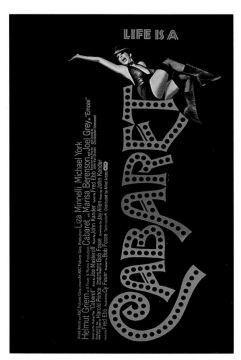

272. BOB FOSSE, Best Director, Cabaret,
1972, one-sheet

273. LIZA MINELLI, Best Actress, Cabaret, 1972,
also JOEL GRAY, Best Supporting Actor, lobby card

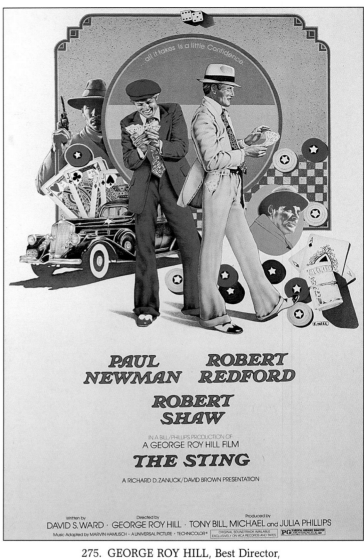

274. THE STING, Best Picture, 1973, one-sheet

275. GEORGE ROY HILL, Best Director, The Sting, 1973, Forty By Sixty

278. JOHN HOUSEMAN, Best Supporting Actor, The Paper Chase, 1973, still

276. JACK LEMMON, Best Actor, Save the Tiger, 1973, one-sheet

277. GLENDA JACKSON, Best Actress, A Touch of Class, 1973, one-sheet

279. TATUM O'NEAL, Best Supporting Actress, Paper Moon, 1973, lobby card

280. THE GODFATHER PART II, Best Picture, 1974, advance one-sheet

281. ELLEN BURSTYN, Best Actress, Alice Doesn't Live Here Anymore, 1974, one-sheet

282. FRANCIS FORD COPPOLA, Best Director, The Godfather Part II, 1974, video poster

283. ART CARNEY, Best Actor, Harry and Tonto, 1974, still

284. ROBERT DeNIRO, Best Supporting Actor, The Godfather Part II, 1974, still

285. INGRID BERGMAN, Best Supporting Actress, Murder on the Orient Express, 1974, lobby card

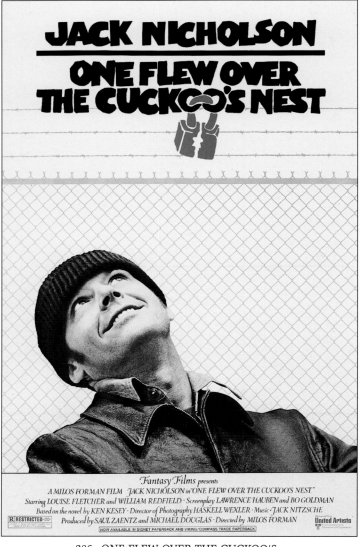

286. ONE FLEW OVER THE CUCKOO'S
NEST, Best Picture, 1975, one-sheet

287. MILOS FORMAN, Best Director,
One Flew Over the Cuckoo's Nest,
1975, lobby card

288. JACK NICHOLSON, Best Actor,
One Flew Over the Cuckoo's Nest,
1975, lobby card

289. LOUISE FLETCHER, Best Actress,
One Flew Over the Cuckoo's Nest, 1975,
lobby card

290. GEORGE BURNS, Best Supporting
Actor, The Sunshine Boys, 1975, lobby card

291. LEE GRANT, Best Supporting Actress,
Shampoo, 1975, lobby card

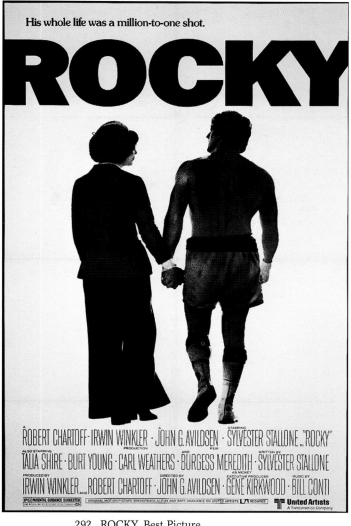

292. ROCKY, Best Picture,
also JOHN G. AVILDSEN, Best Director,
1976, one-sheet

293. FAYE DUNAWAY, Best Actress,
Network, 1976, one-sheet

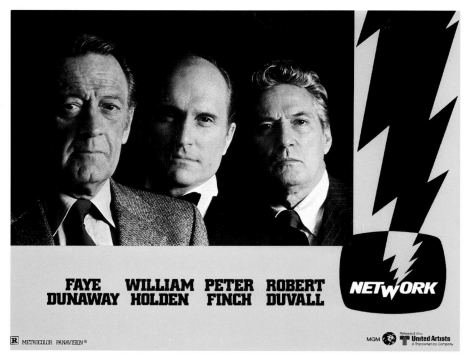

294. PETER FINCH, Best Actor, Network,
1976, lobby card

295. JASON ROBARDS, Best Supporting
Actor, All the President's Men, 1976,
lobby card

296. BEATRICE STRAIGHT, Best
Supporting Actress, Network, 1976, still

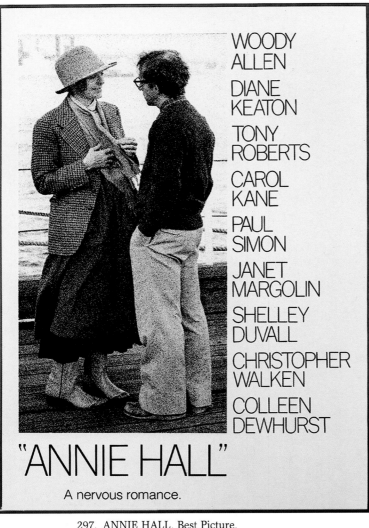

WOODY
ALLEN

DIANE
KEATON

TONY
ROBERTS

CAROL
KANE

PAUL
SIMON

JANET
MARGOLIN

SHELLEY
DUVALL

CHRISTOPHER
WALKEN

COLLEEN
DEWHURST

"ANNIE HALL"

A nervous romance.

297. ANNIE HALL, Best Picture,
also WOODY ALLEN, Best Director, 1977,
one-sheet

Thank you Neil Simon
for making us laugh about
falling in love...
again.

the
Goodbye
Girl

A RAY STARK PRODUCTION OF A HERBERT ROSS FILM
NEIL SIMON'S
"THE GOODBYE GIRL"
RICHARD DREYFUSS · MARSHA MASON
and introducing QUINN CUMMINGS as Lucy
Written by NEIL SIMON · Produced by RAY STARK · Directed by HERBERT ROSS
Music Scored and Adapted by DAVE GRUSIN · Song "Goodbye Girl"
Written and Performed by DAVID GATES · a RASTAR Feature · Prints by MGM Labs.
Now Single Available on Elektra Records | Now Available in Paperback From Warner Books.
From Warner Bros.
A Warner Communications Company

298. RICHARD DREYFUSS, Best Actor,
The Goodbye Girl, 1977, one-sheet

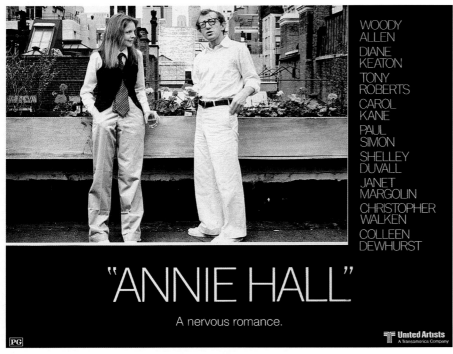

WOODY
ALLEN

DIANE
KEATON

TONY
ROBERTS

CAROL
KANE

PAUL
SIMON

SHELLEY
DUVALL

JANET
MARGOLIN

CHRISTOPHER
WALKEN

COLLEEN
DEWHURST

"ANNIE HALL"

A nervous romance.

PG

United Artists
A Transamerica Company

299. DIANE KEATON, Best Actress,
Annie Hall, 1977, lobby card

The story of two women whose friendship
suddenly became a matter of life and death.

JULIA

Based on a true story.

20th CENTURY-FOX Presents
A RICHARD ROTH Presentation of A FRED ZINNEMANN Film
JANE FONDA   VANESSA REDGRAVE
JULIA
also
starring JASON ROBARDS   HAL HOLBROOK
ROSEMARY MURPHY and MAXIMILIAN SCHELL as "Johann"
Directed by   Produced by   Screenplay by   Based upon the story by
FRED ZINNEMANN   RICHARD ROTH   ALVIN SARGENT   LILLIAN HELLMAN
PG PARENTAL GUIDANCE SUGGESTED
SOME MATERIAL MAY NOT BE SUITABLE FOR CHILDREN
Music by   PRINTS By DeLUXE
GEORGES DELERUE   © 1977 20th Century-Fox

300. JASON ROBARDS, Best Supporting
Actor, Julia, 1977,
also VANESSA REDGRAVE, Best Supporting
Actress, one-sheet

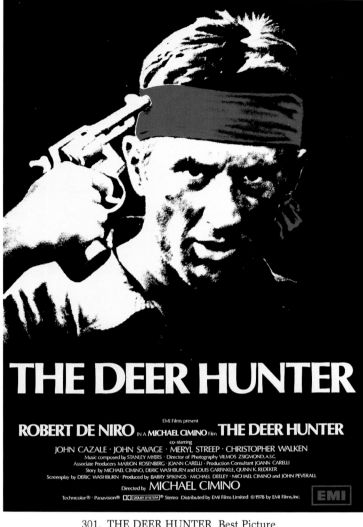

301. THE DEER HUNTER, Best Picture, 1978, one-sheet

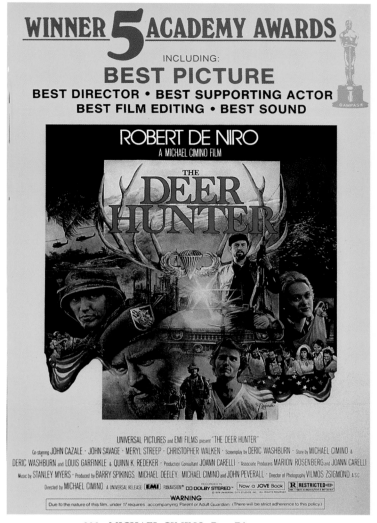

302. MICHAEL CIMINO, Best Director, The Deer Hunter, 1978, "awards" one-sheet

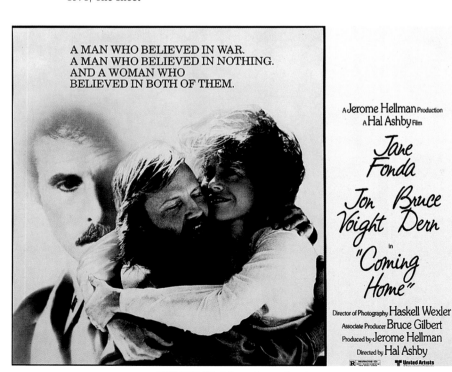

303. JON VOIGHT, Best Actor, Coming Home, 1978, *also* JANE FONDA, Best Actress, half-sheet

304. CHRISTOPHER WALKEN, Best Supporting Actor, The Deer Hunter, 1978, lobby card

305. MAGGIE SMITH, Best Supporting Actress, California Suite, 1978, lobby card

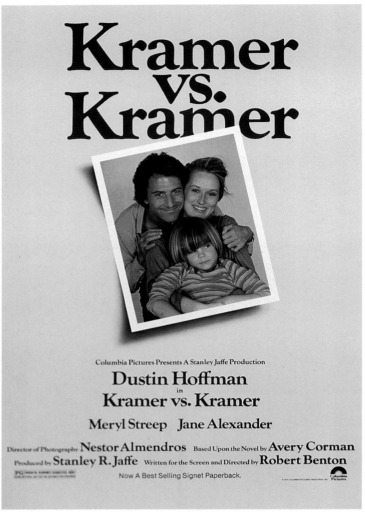

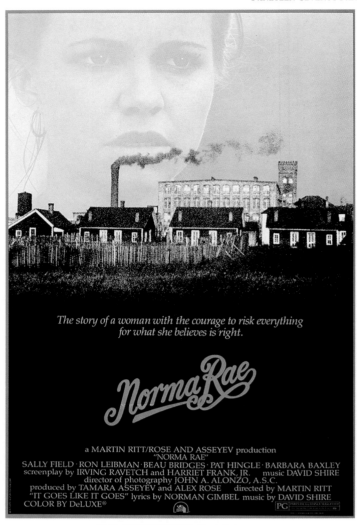

306. KRAMER VS. KRAMER, Best Picture,
also RICHARD BENTON, Best Director,
1979, one-sheet

307. SALLY FIELD, Best Actress,
Norma Rae, 1979, one-sheet

Note: Dustin Hoffman finally received his long overdue
Academy Award in 1979. Melvyn Douglas received a second
Best Supporting Oscar. Douglas had been in films for nearly
half a century and many of his finest performances were
given late in his career.

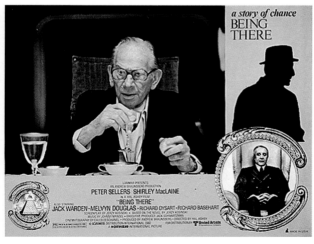

308. DUSTIN HOFFMAN, Best Actor,
Kramer vs. Kramer, 1979,
also MERYL STREEP, Best Supporting
Actress, lobby card

309. MELVYN DOUGLAS, Best Supporting
Actor, Being There, 1979, lobby card

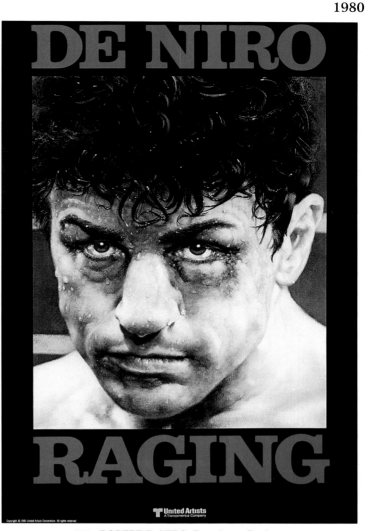

310. ORDINARY PEOPLE, Best Picture, 1980, one-sheet

311. ROBERT DeNIRO, Best Actor, Raging Bull, 1980, advance one-sheet

314. ROBERT REDFORD, Best Director, Ordinary People, 1980, lobby card

312. SISSY SPACEK, Best Actress, Coal Miner's Daughter, 1980, one-sheet

313. MARY STEENBURGEN, Best Supporting Actress, Melvin and Howard, 1980, one-sheet

315. TIMOTHY HUTTON, Best Supporting Actor, Ordinary People, 1980, lobby card

316. CHARIOTS OF FIRE, Best Picture,
1981, one-sheet

317. WARREN BEATTY, Best Director,
Reds, 1981, one-sheet

321. MAUREEN STAPLETON, Best
Supporting Actress, Reds, 1981, still

318, 319. HENRY FONDA, Best Actor,
On Golden Pond, 1981, two lobby cards

320. KATHARINE HEPBURN, Best Actress,
On Golden Pond, 1981, one-sheet

322. JOHN GIELGUD, Best Supporting
Actor, Arthur, 1981, lobby card

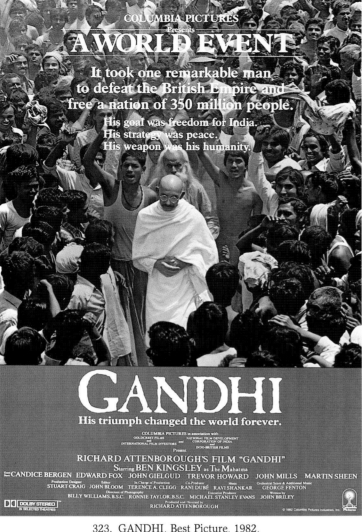

323. GANDHI, Best Picture, 1982, one-sheet

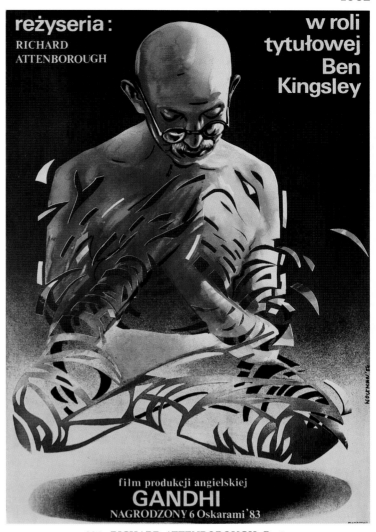

324. RICHARD ATTENBOROUGH, Best Director, Gandhi, 1982, Polish poster

Note: 1982 seemed to mark a turning point for the Academy Awards. Whereas in 1981 all the acting Awards went to performers with long distinguished careers, in 1982 they went to performers who were just beginning. Perhaps the Academy recognized that if it would acknowledge deserving performances when they were given, there would be no need to give "consolation" Awards to make up for earlier omissions.

327. LOUIS GOSSETT, JR., Best Supporting Actor, An Officer and a Gentleman, 1982, Spanish lobby card

325. BEN KINGSLEY, Best Actor, Gandhi, 1982, still

326. MERYL STREEP, Best Actress, Sophie's Choice, 1982, one-sheet

328. JESSICA LANGE, Best Supporting Actress, Tootsie, 1982, lobby card

329. TERMS OF ENDEARMENT, Best Picture,
also JAMES L. BROOKS, Best Director,
1983, one-sheet

330. ROBERT DUVALL, Best Actor, Tender Mercies, 1983, one-sheet

331. SHIRLEY MacLAINE, Best Actress, Terms of Endearment, 1983, lobby card

332. JACK NICHOLSON, Best Supporting Actor, Terms of Endearment, 1983, lobby card

333. LINDA HUNT, Best Supporting Actress, The Year of Living Dangerously, 1983, lobby card

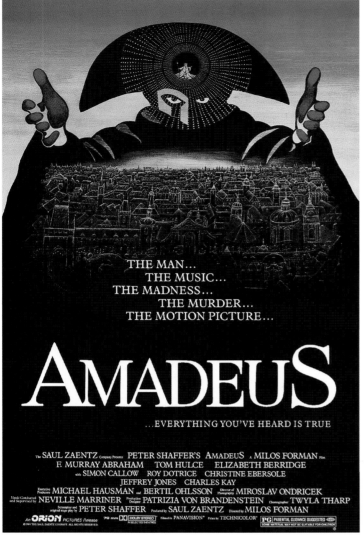

334. AMADEUS, Best Picture, 1984,
one-sheet

335. MILOS FORMAN, Best Director,
Amadeus, 1984, lobby card

Note: It is often said that winning an Academy Award is of incalculable benefit to an actor's career, yet sadly this has not been the case for F. Murray Abraham. Although he is a superlative actor, the last decade's emphasis on youth and action films has not provided him with memorable roles.

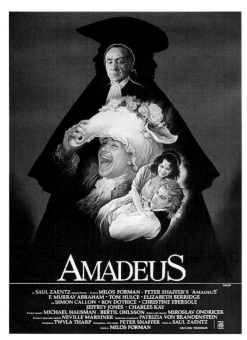

336. F. MURRAY ABRAHAM, Best Actor,
Amadeus, 1984, Italian poster

337. SALLY FIELD, Best Actress, Places in
the Heart, 1984, one-sheet

338. HAING S. NGOR, Best Supporting
Actor, The Killing Fields, 1984, lobby card

339. PEGGY ASHCROFT, Best Supporting
Actress, A Passage to India, 1984, lobby
card

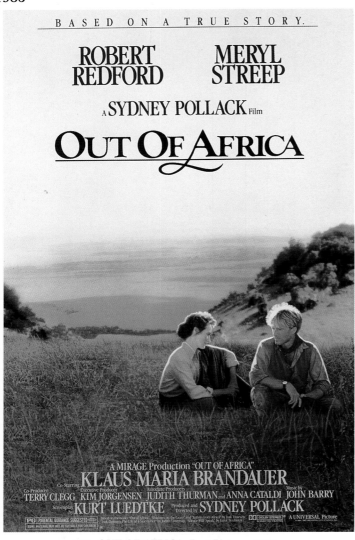

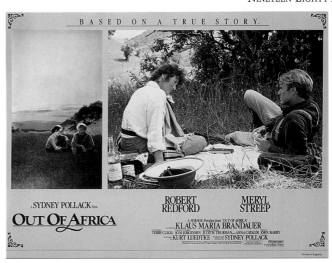

340. OUT OF AFRICA, Best Picture, 1985,
one-sheet

341, 342. SYDNEY POLLACK, Best Director,
Out of Africa, 1985, two lobby cards

345. DON AMECHE, Best Supporting Actor,
Cocoon, 1985, still

343. WILLIAM HURT, Best Actor, Kiss of
the Spider Woman, 1985, still

344. GERALDINE PAGE, Best Actress,
The Trip to Bountiful, 1985, one-sheet

346. ANGELICA HUSTON, Best Supporting
Actress, Prizzi's Honor, 1985, still

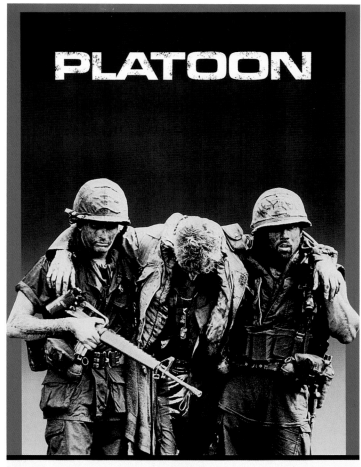

347. PLATOON, Best Picture, 1986,
one-sheet

348. OLIVER STONE, Best Director,
Platoon, 1986, one-sheet

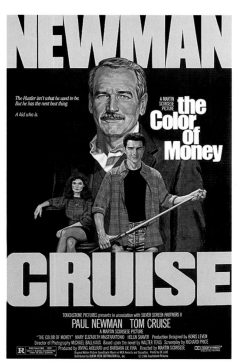

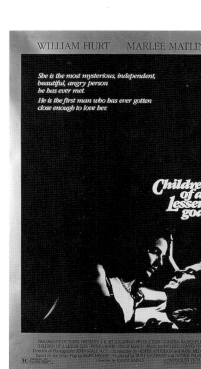

351. MICHAEL CAINE, Best Supporting
Actor, Hannah and Her Sisters, 1986, still

349. PAUL NEWMAN, Best Actor,
The Color of Money, 1986, one-sheet

350. MARLEE MATLIN, Best Actress,
Children of a Lesser God, 1986, one-sheet

352. DIANNE WIEST, Best Supporting
Actress, Hannah and Her Sisters, 1986, still

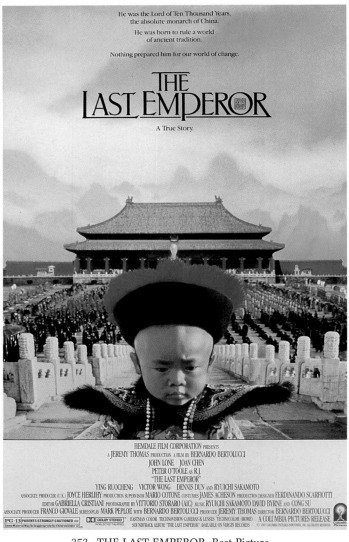

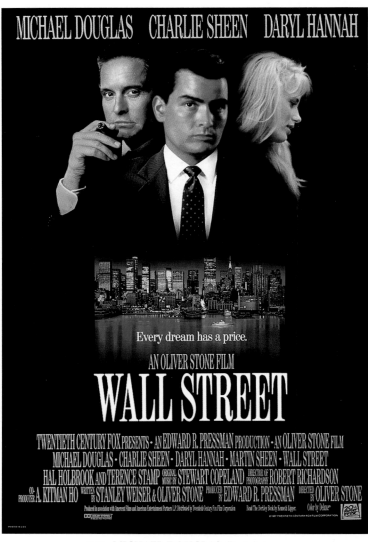

353. THE LAST EMPEROR, Best Picture, *also* BERNARDO BERTOLUCCI, Best Director, 1987, one-sheet

354. MICHAEL DOUGLAS, Best Actor, Wall Street, 1987, one-sheet

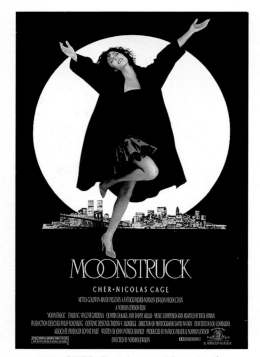

355. CHER, Best Actress, Moonstruck, 1987, one-sheet

356. SEAN CONNERY, Best Supporting Actor, The Untouchables, 1987, one-sheet

357, 358. OLYMPIA DUKAKIS, Best Supporting Actress, Moonstruck, 1987, two lobby cards

359. RAIN MAN, Best Picture,
also BARRY LEVINSON, Best Director,
also DUSTIN HOFFMAN, Best Actor, 1988,
one-sheet

360. JODIE FOSTER, Best Actress,
The Accused, 1988, one-sheet

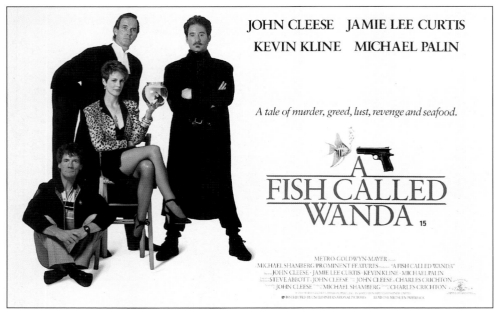

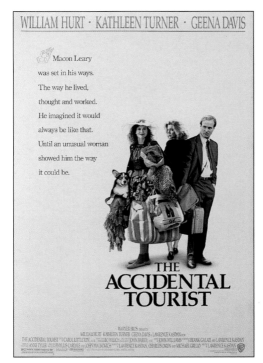

361. KEVIN KLINE, Best Supporting Actor,
A Fish Called Wanda, 1988, British quad
poster

362. GEENA DAVIS, Best Supporting
Actress, The Accidental Tourist, 1988,
one-sheet

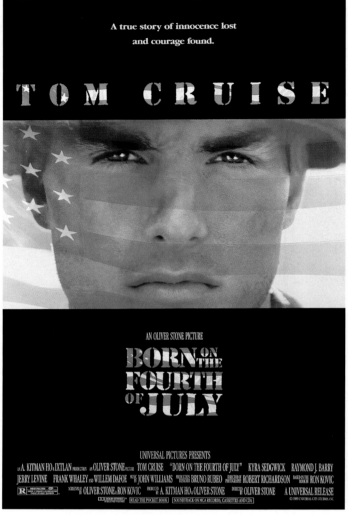

363. DRIVING MISS DAISY, Best Picture, 1989, one-sheet

364. OLIVER STONE, Best Director, Born on the Fourth of July, 1989, one-sheet

Note: The end of the 1980s saw a recent trend in Academy voting firmly established. It seems the Academy was finally putting sentiment aside and recognize those who, in its opinion, truly had delivered the best performance, regardless of the age of the performer and whether they had won before.

Unfortunately, a recent trend of movie posters also seem firmly established. Film makers were only making a single style one-sheet for the domestic release of most films, with virtually no other sizes, except banners and standees.

367. BRENDA FRICKER, Best Supporting Actress, My Left Foot, 1989, still

365. DANIEL DAY LEWIS, Best Actor, My Left Foot, 1989, still

366. JESSICA TANDY, Best Actress, Driving Miss Daisy, 1989, still

368. DENZEL WASHINGTON, Best Supporting Actor, Glory, 1989, lobby card

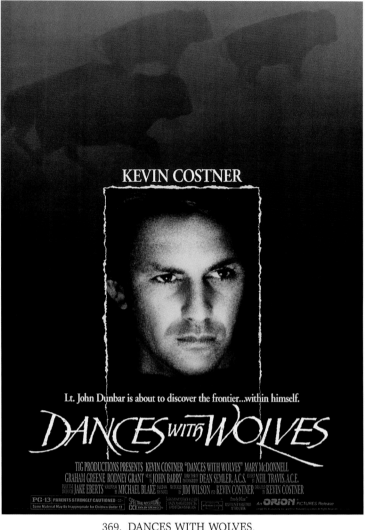

369. DANCES WITH WOLVES,
Best Picture, 1990, one-sheet

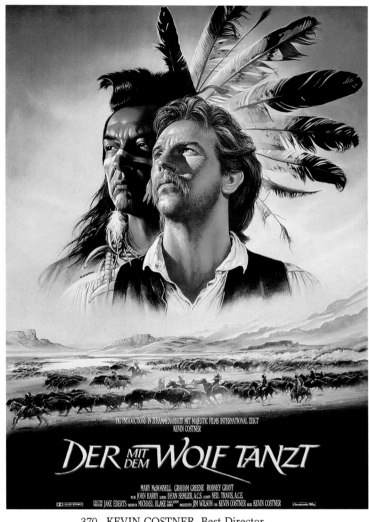

370. KEVIN COSTNER, Best Director,
Dances With Wolves, 1990, German poster

371. JEREMY IRONS, Best Actor, Reversal
of Fortune, 1990, one-sheet

372. KATHY BATES, Best Actress, Misery,
1990, still

373. WHOOPI GOLDBERG, Best
Supporting Actress, Ghost, 1990, still

374. JOE PESCI, Best Supporting Actor,
GoodFellas, 1990, one-sheet

375. THE SILENCE OF THE LAMBS, Best
Picture,
also JONATHAN DEMME, Best Director,
1991, one-sheet

376. ANTHONY HOPKINS, Best Actor,
The Silence of the Lambs, 1991, one-sheet

378. JACK PALANCE, Best Supporting
Actor, City Slickers, 1991, still

377. JODIE FOSTER, Best Actress,
The Silence of the Lambs, 1991,
German lobby card

379. MERCEDES RUEHL, Best Supporting
Actress, The Fisher King, 1991, lobby card

380. UNFORGIVEN, Best Picture, 1992,
one-sheet

381. CLINT EASTWOOD, Best Director,
Unforgiven, 1992,
also GENE HACKMAN, Best Supporting
Actor, one-sheet

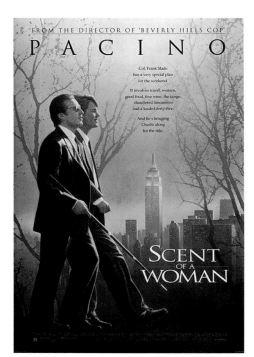

Note: *Howard's End* received a full scale major
theatrical release, unlike earlier
Merchant/Ivory productions. The producers
were afraid to advertise its theme of middle
age romance (shades of *Dodsworth* over a half
a century earlier) and amazingly did not
picture either Anthony Hopkins or Emma
Thompson on the one-sheet poster!

382. AL PACINO, Best Actor, Scent of a
Woman, 1992, one-sheet

383. EMMA THOMPSON, Best Actress,
Howard's End, 1992, still

384. MARISA TOMEI, Best Supporting
Actress, My Cousin Vinny, 1992, one-sheet

385. SCHINDLER'S LIST, Best Picture,
also STEVEN SPIELBERG, Best Director,
1993, one-sheet

386. HOLLY HUNTER, Best Actress,
The Piano, 1993, one-sheet

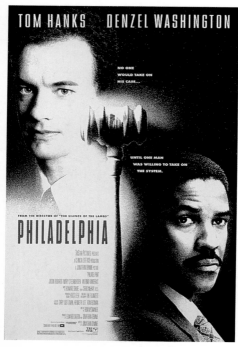

Note: After over sixty years, the Academy has continued to grow and evolve, which accounts for its pre-eminence among all awards presentations. While one may argue over who won in any given acting category (and certainly there have been numerous ferocious arguments), it seems clear the members are voting for who they believe truly gave the best performance that particular year, without regard to past performances. Let us hope the Academy keeps to these guidelines, so that the "Best" is truly the best!

387. TOM HANKS, Best Actor,
Philadelphia, 1993, one-sheet

388. TOMMY LEE JONES, Best Supporting
Actor, The Fugitive, 1993, still

389. ANNA PACQUIN, Best Supporting
Actress, The Piano, 1993, still

390. FORREST GUMP, Best Picture, *also* ROBERT ZEMECKIS, Best Director, 1994, one-sheet

391. TOM HANKS, Best Actor, Forrest Gump, 1994, still

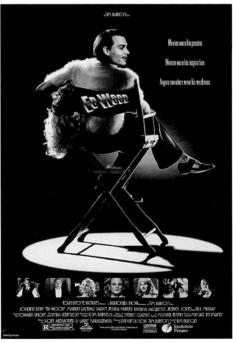

392. JESSICA LANGE, Best Actress, Blue Sky, 1994, one-sheet

393. DIANNE WEIST, Best Supporting Actress, Bullets Over Broadway, 1994, one-sheet

394. MARTIN LANDAU, Best Supporting Actor, Ed Wood, 1994, one-sheet

ACADEMY AWARD® WINNERS' MOVIE POSTERS INDEX

BEST PICTURES

All About Eve 126
All Quiet on the Western Front 15
All the King's Men 121
Amadeus 334
An American in Paris 134
Annie Hall .297
The Apartment 194
Around the World in 80 Days . . .167, 168
Ben-Hur 186
The Best Years of Our Lives 104
The Bridge on the River Kwai 174
The Broadway Melody 11
Casablanca .87
Cavalcade 28
Chariots of Fire 316
Cimarron 19
Dances With Wolves 369
The Deer Hunter 301
Driving Miss Daisy 363
Forrest Gump 390
The French Connection 264
From Here to Eternity 148
Gandhi 323
Gentleman's Agreement 109
Gigi 178
The Godfather 269
The Godfather Part II 280
Going My Way 93
Gone With the Wind 63
Grand Hotel 23
The Greatest Show on Earth 141, 142
The Great Ziegfeld 45
Hamlet 115
How Green Was My Valley 76
In the Heat of the Night 238
It Happened One Night 33
Kramer vs. Kramer 306
The Last Emperor 353
Lawrence of Arabia 207
The Life of Emile Zola 51
The Lost Weekend 99
A Man for All Seasons 234
Marty 160
Midnight Cowboy 252
Mrs. Miniver 82
Mutiny on the Bounty 40, 42
My Fair Lady 220
Oliver! 246
One Flew Over the Cuckoo's Nest . . .286
On the Waterfront 154
Ordinary People 310
Out of Africa 340
Patton 258
Platoon 347
Rain Man 359
Rebecca 70
Rocky 292
Schindler's List 385
The Silence of the Lambs 375
The Sound of Music 227
The Sting 274
Terms of Endearment 329
Tom Jones .213
Unforgiven 380
West Side Story 201
Wings 1, 2, 3
You Can't Take It With You 57

INDIVIDUALS

(Those winning multiple awards are noted
in parentheses)

F. Murray Abraham 336
Jack Albertson 250
Woody Allen 297
Don Ameche 345
Julie Andrews 224
George Arliss 18
Peggy Ashcroft 339
Mary Astor .81
Richard Attenborough 324
John G. Avildsen 292
Fay Bainter .61
Martin Balsam 232
Anne Bancroft 210
Ethel Barrymore 98

Lionel Barrymore 20
Kathy Bates 372
Anne Baxter 108
Warner Baxter 13
Warren Beatty 317
Wallace Beery 25
Ed Begley .211
Robert Benton 306
Ingrid Bergman (3) 96, 171, 285
Bernardo Bertolucci 353
Humphrey Bogart 137
Shirley Booth 145
Ernest Borgnine 162
Frank Borzage (2) 4, 24
Alice Brady .56
Marlon Brando (2) 156, 270
Walter Brennan (3) 49, 62, 71
James L. Brooks 329
Yul Brynner 170
George Burns 290
Red Buttons 178
Ellen Burstyn 281
James Cagney 84
Michael Caine 351
Frank Capra (3) 34, 46, 59
Art Carney .283
George Chakiris 205
Cher 355
Julie Christie 231
Michael Cimino 302
Charles Coburn 91
Claudette Colbert 36–39
Ronald Colman 111
Sean Connery 356
Gary Cooper (2) 77, 144
Francis Ford Coppola 282
Kevin Costner 370
Broderick Crawford 121
Joan Crawford 101
Donald Crisp 80
Bing Crosby 95
George Cukor 221, 222
Michael Curtiz 88
Jane Darwell 72
Bette Davis (2) 43, 58
Geena Davis 362
Olivia de Havilland (2) 106, 123
Jonathan Demme 375
Sandy Dennis 236
Robert DeNiro (2) 284, 311
Robert Donat 65
Melvyn Douglas (2) 217, 309
Michael Douglas 354
Marie Dressler 22
Richard Dreyfuss 298
Olympia Dukakis 357, 358
Patty Duke 212
Faye Dunaway 293
James Dunn 102
Robert Duvall 330
Clint Eastwood 381
Jose Ferrer 129, 130
Sally Field (2) 307, 337
Peter Finch 294
Barry Fitzgerald 97
Victor Fleming 64
Louise Fletcher 289
Henry Fonda 318, 319
Jane Fonda (2) 266, 267, 303
Joan Fontaine 78
John Ford (4) 41, 69, 74, 79, 143
Milos Forman (2) 287, 335
Bob Fosse .272
Jodie Foster (2) 360, 377
Brenda Fricker 367
William Friedkin 264
Clark Gable .35
Greer Garson 83
Janet Gaynor 5, 7, 9
John Gielgud 322
Whoopi Goldberg 373
Ruth Gordon 251
Louis Gossett, Jr. 327
Gloria Grahame 147
Lee Grant .291

Joel Grey 273
Hugh Griffith 192
Alec Guinness 175
Edmund Gwenn 114
Gene Hackman (2) 265, 381
Tom Hanks (2) 387, 391
Rex Harrison 223
Goldie Hawn 257
Helen Hayes (2) 27, 263
Susan Hayward 183
Eileen Heckart 271
Van Heflin 85
Audrey Hepburn 152
Katharine Hepburn (4) . .30, 242, 243, 248,
320
Charlton Heston 189, 190
George Roy Hill 275
Wendy Hiller 185
Dustin Hoffman (2) 308, 359
William Holden 150, 151
Judy Holliday 131
Celeste Holm 113
Anthony Hopkins 376
John Houseman 278
Josephine Hull 133
Linda Hunt 333
Holly Hunter 386
Kim Hunter 140
William Hurt 343
Angelica Huston 346
John Huston 116
Walter Huston 120
Timothy Hutton 315
Jeremy Irons 371
Burl Ives 184
Glenda Jackson (2) 261, 277
Dean Jagger 124
Emil Jannings 8, 10
Ben Johnson 268
Jennifer Jones 89
Shirley Jones 200
Tommy Lee Jones (2) 388
Elia Kazan (2) 110, 155
Diane Keaton 299
Lila Kedrova 226
Grace Kelly 157
George Kennedy 244
Ben Kingsley 325
Kevin Kline 361
Burt Lancaster 198
Jessica Lange (2) 328, 392
Charles Laughton 31, 32
Martin Landau 394
Cloris Leachman 268
David Lean (2) 176, 208
Vivien Leigh (2) 66, 138
Jack Lemmon (2) 165, 276
Barry Levinson 359
Daniel Day Lewis 365
Frank Lloyd (2) 12, 29
Sophia Loren 204
Paul Lukas .90
Mercedes McCambridge 125
Leo McCarey (2) 52, 94
Hattie McDaniel 67
Victor McLaglen 44
Shirley MacLaine 331
Anna Magnani 163, 164
Karl Malden 139
Dorothy Malone 173
Joseph L. Mankiewicz (2) . . .122, 127, 128
Delbert Mann 161
Fredric March (2) 26, 105
Lee Marvin 230
Marlee Matlin 350
Walter Matthau 237
Lewis Milestone (2) 6, 17
Ray Milland 100
John Mills .262
Liza Minelli 273
Vincente Minnelli 180, 181
Thomas Mitchell 68
Rita Moreno 206
Paul Muni 47
Patricia Neal 215

Paul Newman 349
Haing S. Ngor 338
Mike Nichols 239, 240
Jack Nicholson (2) 288, 332
David Niven 182
Edmund O'Brien 158
Laurence Olivier 117
Tatum O'Neal 279
Al Pacino 382
Anna Pacquin 389
Geraldine Page 344
Jack Palance 378
Estelle Parsons 245
Katina Paxinou 92
Gregory Peck 209
Joe Pesci 374
Mary Pickford 14
Sidney Poitier 216
Sidney Pollack 341, 342
Anthony Quinn (2) 146, 172
Luise Rainer (2) 48, 54
Robert Redford 314
Carol Reed 246
Donna Reed 153
Ann Revere 103
Vanessa Redgrave 300
Tony Richardson 214
Jason Robards (2) 295, 300
Jerome Robbins 202
Cliff Robertson 247
Ginger Rogers 73
Mercedes Ruehl 379
Harold Russell 107
Margaret Rutherford 218, 219
George Sanders 132
Eva Marie Saint 159
Franklin J. Schaffner 259
Maximillian Schell 203
Joseph Schildkraut 55
John Schlesinger 254
Paul Scofield 235
George C. Scott 260
Norma Shearer 16
Frank Sinatra 153
Simone Signoret 191
Maggie Smith (2) 255, 305
Gale Sondergaard 50
Sissy Spacek 312
Steven Spielberg 385
Maureen Stapleton 321
Mary Steenburgen 313
Rod Steiger 241
George Stevens (2) 135, 136, 169
James Stewart 75
Oliver Stone (2) 348, 364
Beatrice Straight 296
Meryl Streep (2) 308, 326
Barbra Streisand 249
Jessica Tandy 366
Norman Taurog 21
Elizabeth Taylor (2) 195, 236
Emma Thompson 383
Marisa Tomei 384
Spencer Tracy (2) 53, 60
Claire Trevor 118
Miyoshi Umeki 178
Peter Ustinov (2) 199, 225
Jo Van Fleet 166
Jon Voight .303
Christopher Walken 304
Denzel Washington 368
John Wayne 253
Dianne Weist (2) 352, 393
Shelley Winters (2) 193, 233
Robert Wise (2) 202, 228, 229
Joanne Woodward 177
Teresa Wright 86
Billy Wilder (2) 99, 196, 197
William Wyler (3) 82, 104, 187, 188
Jane Wyman 119
Gig Young .256
Loretta Young 112
Robert Zemeckis 390
Fred Zinnemann (2) 149, 234